WISDOM FOR KIDS

BOOK 1: The Purpose of Proverbs

ADAPTED BY: T.L. Martínez   ILLUSTRATED BY: James Koenig

Wisdom For Kids - Book 1: The Purpose of Proverbs

By Tito and Liz Martínez

Copyright © 2021 by Tito and Liz Martínez - www.lionstalesbooks.com

Illustrations by James Koenig - www.freelancefridge.com

Coloring by Marshal Uhls - www.marshaluhls.artstation.com

ISBN 978-1-7369409-1-4

tlmartinez@lionstalesbooks.com

For Enzo and Kate. May the Lord bless you and keep you. May he make his face shine upon you and be gracious to you. May he give you his favor and give you his peace.

- T.L. Martínez -

To my future children, we pray for you every day and look forward to seeing the amazing children of God you will become.

- James Koenig -

A Note To Parents:

As Christian parents, we are always seeking to bring God's word to life for our own children. Both of us grew up reading Proverbs as children in family devotions – each in our native languages. In writing this series, we sought to find a creative way to present the book of Proverbs to our kids, personifying the character traits described throughout Proverbs.

As a bilingual family, we referenced several versions of the Bible in both English and Spanish to help us write each book. Our goal in this series is to adapt each chapter of Proverbs, verse by verse, line by line – not leaving out anything but simply making it fun and understandable for even the youngest children.

And you must commit yourselves wholeheartedly to these commands that I am giving you today. Repeat them again and again to your children. Talk about them when you are at home and when you are on the road, when you are going to bed and when you are getting up. Tie them to your hands and wear them on your forehead as reminders. Write them on the doorposts of your house and on your gates. (Deut. 6:6-9)

Hi Kids! I'm Solomon, King of Israel. When I was young, I asked God for wisdom, and He made me the wisest man that ever lived. I wrote this book as a manual for living a life of wisdom. This book will help you understand what life means and where it's going.

This guide will teach you how to be wise and how to have understanding and self-control (stuff we all need).

You'll learn what is honest, fair, and right when you read these instructions. Since you're young and inexperienced in life, it will help you learn the ropes. Getting knowledge and good sense will give you a strong grasp on reality to help you navigate your life.

Even the wisest person in the world can learn from this guide!
Everyone can find direction and good advice in these words.

The first step toward wisdom is learning to respect the Lord.
Only silly people hate wisdom and discipline - don't be like that!

Pay close attention to what your father tells you and don't forget your mother's advice - they tell you a lot, I'm sure!

Their teaching will turn your life into something truly beautiful.
Their advice will be like flowers in your hair or a crown on your head.
They'll really make you stand out in the crowd.

If you have bad friends who try to convince you to do bad things, don't even give them a second look. Don't listen to them for a minute — and whatever you do, don't go with them!

They are racing towards a dead end, hurrying to ruin everything they get their hands on. They're only setting their own trap, like an accident waiting to happen.

They act this way because they want to get things they haven't worked for.

This kind of greed really sucks the life out of you –

the more you have, the less you are.

Instead of listening to bad friends, look for Captain Wisdom.
She walks around town calling out to anyone who will listen to her.

"Hey, Kids!" she says, "Where are you headed? Don't you want to learn about wisdom and knowledge? I can help you live your life. I'll pour out my heart to you and make you wise!"

I've called, but you've refused to listen. I held out my hand, but you didn't pay attention. You didn't follow my advice, and you didn't listen to my correction. So, I won't get involved when you get in trouble.

What if the roof falls in, and your whole life goes to pieces? Trouble will overtake you like a storm. Pain and suffering will overwhelm you, and you will look for me then.

You will look for me when you are in trouble, but you won't find me if you never took the time to listen to my advice and correction. If you hate knowledge and choose not to respect the Lord — if you choose your own path and not the way of Wisdom - you will never find me.

Don't you see what happens? When you don't listen and don't care, you will be destroyed.

But all who choose to listen to me, Captain Wisdom, will live in peace and safety, without the fear of being hurt. You can take it easy — you're in good hands.

About The Authors:

Tito and Liz Martínez live in Houston, TX with their two children. Tito is a native of San Salvador, El Salvador while Liz is a transplanted Houstonian. The couple met in church in 2008 and married on top of the Quezaltepeque volcano (El Boquerón) in San Salvador in 2013. Liz owns her own children's services agency and holds a Master of Educational Psychology from the University of Houston, while Tito runs his own marketing company and studied Theology at Universidad Evangélica de El Salvador. As the founders of Lion's Tales, Wisdom for Kids is their first series of children's books.

Author email:

tlmartinez@lionstalesbooks.com

Website:

www.lionstalesbooks.com

About The Illustrator and Colorist:

James Koenig and Marshal Uhls have worked together on projects for many years. They originally teamed up on a large character development line with a tight deadline. They quickly discovered they enjoyed collaborating and have grown into a great team, creating spectacular books and designs together. James illustrates the pages and Marshal colors the drawings.

James has illustrated 50 children's books (and counting) and has created characters and illustrations for countless other children's toys and products over the last 15 years.

Marshal has illustrated for video games and other products for over 10 years. He has a knack for matching the illustration styles that James creates. The vibrancy he creates while coloring brings out the best in the books they work on together.

You can learn more about them at: www.freelancefridge.com.

We were inspired by the following translations of the Bible in our writings:

References:

Biblia para todos: Traducción en lenguaje actual. (2003). Brasil: Sociedades Bíblicas Unidas.

Holy Bible: International Children's Bible. (1999). Nashville, TN: Tommy Nelson.

Holy Bible. New Living Translation. (2005). Wheaton, IL: Tyndale House.

La Biblia: Dios Habla Hoy. (2013). Sociedades Bíblicas Unidas.

La Palabra de Dios Para Todos: La Biblia de las Américas. (1975). México: The Lockman Foundation.

La Santa Biblia: Nueva Versión Internacional. (2004). Miami, FL: Sociedad Bíblica Internacional.

The Holy Bible: King James version. (2014). Peabody, MA: Hendrickson.

The Holy Bible, New International Version. (1984). Grand Rapids: Zondervan Publishing House.

The Message. (2004). Colorado Springs, CO: NavPress.

Santa Biblia: Antiguo y Nuevo Testamento. (2016). Nashville, TN: Holman Bible.

Santa Biblia: Nueva Traducción Viviente. (2018). Carol Stream, IL: Tyndale House.

Young's Literal Translation of the Holy Bible. (1977). Grand Rapids, MI: Baker Book House.

Collect all the books in the Wisdom for Kids series.

All books are available on:

 • **BARNES & NOBLE** • Bookshop •

... and many other places you purchase books online!

BOOK 1: The Purpose of Proverbs
in English

LIBRO 1: El Propósito de los Proverbios
en Español

BOOK 2: Wisdom Has Rewards!
in English

LIBRO 2: La Sabiduría Tiene Recompensas
en Español

Made in the USA
Middletown, DE
16 January 2022